P9-EDV-659

THE WORLD'S WEATHER

DAVID FLINT

Thomson Learning • New York

Young Geographer

First published in the
United States in 1993 by
Thomson Learning
115 Fifth Avenue
New York, NY 10003

First published in 1992 by
Wayland (Publishers) Ltd

Copyright © 1992 Wayland (Publishers) Ltd

U.S. revision copyright © 1993 Thomson Learning

Cataloging-in-Publication Data applied for

ISBN: 1-56847-053-3

Printed in Italy

Contents

All the words that are in **bold** appear in the glossary on page 30.

Introduction

Different parts of the earth have different kinds of weather. Some places like North Africa are hot, while others like Greenland are cold. Some places like the rain forest of Brazil are wet, while others like the Sahara are dry. The world's weather varies from place to place and this affects the people, plants, and animals that live in those places.

Often weather makes the world's news. This is usually when there are big **storms** such as hurricanes and typhoons or long droughts when plants die. Every day millions of people need to know the weather forecast. They may be farmers wanting to decide the best time to harvest a crop, or fishermen concerned about a storm with very strong winds and heavy rain.

In the fishing industry the weather forecast is vital. This trawler is riding out a severe gale at sea. When the weather improves fishing can start again.

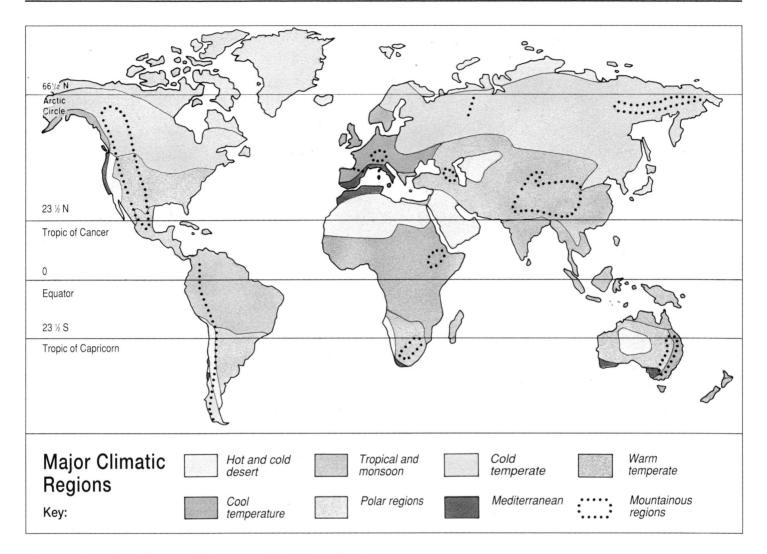

Major Climatic Regions

Key:

| | Hot and cold desert | | Tropical and monsoon | | Cold temperate | | Warm temperate |
| | Cool temperature | | Polar regions | | Mediterranean | ..... | Mountainous regions |

A map showing the world's many different climates

The word "weather" describes the sunshine, cloud cover, wind, rain, and temperature that occur in one place. In many parts of the world, the weather changes a lot from day to day. In other parts, near the **equator** for example, the weather may be the same for weeks. The weather that is usual in a region is called its **climate**.

All the world's weather is the combination of wind, water, and the heat from the sun. These work together to give us a variety of conditions from Arctic cold to tropical heat. The winds carry the water that forms the clouds, rain, and snow. They also help to carry the warmth of the sun to different parts of the earth.

Tropical weather

On either side of the equator lie the **tropics**. These are the areas that lie between the Tropic of Capricorn and the Tropic of Cancer. They have very hot weather because the sun is right overhead much of the year. However, the weather is not the same all over the tropics.

Some areas of the tropics, called "tropical wet climates," have heavy rain for most of the year. They lie close to the equator. "Tropical dry climates" have a wet season followed by a dry season. They lie farther from the equator near the Tropic of Cancer and the Tropic of Capricorn.

Amazon forest

A typical day in the Amazon forest of Brazil starts bright and sunny with very few clouds in the sky. It soon starts to feel hot, but clouds soon build up during the morning. By mid-afternoon it is overcast, with some tall black clouds growing bigger and bigger.

Later in the afternoon there is thunder and lightning together with a heavy downpour of rain, which soaks everything.

When it starts to feel a little cooler, the clouds break up, and evenings are often bright. The weather feels very humid all day although the nights are cooler.

Every day, rain clouds build up over the Amazon forest.

The Andes mountains of South America have cooler weather than nearby lowlands.

In tropical wet climates, the weather is hot and very wet. Annual rainfall is usually more than 60 inches, and afternoon temperatures are usually 85°F to 90°F and higher.

When it is so hot and wet the weather feels very "close" or **humid** all day, even though nights are cooler. In a few places, sea breezes make the weather less humid. In the mountains, the weather is cooler because the place is higher up.

The sun's heating is greatest at the equator. As the air becomes hotter it rises, just like a hot-air balloon. As the air rises, it cools and the moisture in it **condenses** to form water droplets in clouds. The clouds grow during the day, becoming taller and darker. The droplets grow larger, and more of them form as the warm air rises and cools. The droplets finally get so heavy that they fall as rain, often accompanied by thunder and lighting.

As we have seen, tropical dry climates have both wet and dry seasons. There is a big difference in the weather between these seasons. In the wet season, there is lots of heat from the sun. This causes the air to rise, so days start sunny but soon cloud over. Later in the day, dark thunder clouds bring heavy rainstorms which clear only as darkness falls.

In the dry season it is cooler (about 70°F), so days stay bright, clear, sunny, and above all, dry.

In the dry season in tropical dry climates, the grass becomes parched.

West Africa

In West Africa the dry season is cool, clear and often windy. Local people enjoy the cooler temperature but dislike the dust. The Harmattan is a cool, dusty wind blowing from the Sahara. Europeans who went to live in West Africa in the nineteenth century called the wind the "African doctor" because they believed it made them feel better.

The weather in the wet season is hot and sticky. The rainfall often comes in very heavy showers of thunderstorms, which can last for several hours. The heavy rain can cause rivers to burst their banks and flood the nearby land.

A tropical storm brings thunder, lightning, and heavy rain.

A few white clouds may form in the afternoon but these rarely bring any rain.

Tropical dry areas have tall grassland with a few scattered trees.

Most trees cannot survive the dry season. The grass is able to survive by dying back to its roots. Then when the rain returns it starts to grow new shoots.

Desert weather

Deserts are dry places because they have very little rain. Usually they have less than 10 inches of rain in a year, but this figure varies a lot from year to year.

In some deserts it may not rain at all for several years. Then there may be a sudden heavy downpour in the three-month rainy season. These brief, violent storms may cause sudden flooding.

After the rain, some deserts bloom as the cacti and other plants burst into colorful flower. These hardy plants have to complete their life cycle in a very short time when there is water around. Many of them have developed ways of surviving the long drought. But in some places deserts are bare sand or sometimes rock or pebbles because nothing can survive.

Sand dunes like these form the surface of many of the world's deserts. The ripples on the dunes are caused by the wind, which can quickly whip the sand into a fierce storm.

The desert flowers bloom after a rare rainstorm.

During the day in a hot desert the temperature soars. **Thermometers** have shown readings of over 135°F in the Sahara and in Death Valley in California. Sometimes the desert rocks become so hot they will burn anyone who accidentally touches them.

At night, because there are no clouds to hold the heat in, deserts become very cold. Temperatures can drop to 30°F or even colder. People camping out have to wrap up well against the cold. This has given rise to the old saying "night is the winter of the tropics."

Monsoon weather

The word "monsoon" comes from the Arabic word for season. A monsoon is a wind system that reverses its direction twice a year, bringing major weather changes, especially heavy rains.

In monsoon areas the wind blows for six months from the northeast. Then it turns around and blows for six months from the southwest. This reversal can happen in a day.

In India and Pakistan there is a cool, dry season when winds are blowing from the northeast; a hot, dry season as the winds start to shift; and a very wet season when the winds blow from the southwest, carrying moisture from the oceans. Other areas affected by monsoons are southern Asia, parts of Africa, and northern Australia, where rains also come as warm wet winds blow in from the sea.

Monsoon winds change direction, because of changes in **air pressure**, in the middle of large landmasses such as Asia and Australia.

These farmers are wearing capes to protect them from the heavy rain in India.

In the winter the land in these areas quickly loses heat, turns cold, and become a center of high pressure. Winds then blow out from the land to the sea.

In the summer the reverse happens. The land is heated, becoming a center of low pressure. Winds are then drawn in from the sea bringing heavy rain.

The monsoon in India

In India, the cool season lasts from November to January, when the temperature is about 60°F in places like Delhi. The winds are blowing outward from northwestern India and this keeps the country cool and dry.

Between February and May is India's hot season, when the temperature reaches about 100°F in the shade. The sky is usually clear with few clouds and there is no rain.

The rainy season lasts from June to October. During this time the winds change direction and blow into northwest India from across the Indian Ocean. These monsoon winds bring heavy rainfall to the country.

The monsoon starts or "breaks" on June 5 in Bombay, and then moves north, breaking in Calcutta on June 13 and in Delhi on June 30. These dates do not usually alter from year to year.

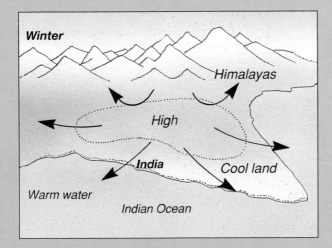

In winter the cool land of northern India becomes an area of high pressure, so dry winds blow outward from the land.

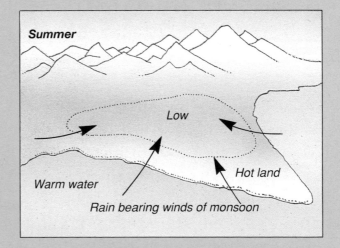

In summer the hot land of northern India becomes an area of low pressure, so warm moist winds blow in from the sea.

Heavy monsoon rains can bring serious flooding to places like Bangladesh.

The monsoon is vital to life in places like India, Pakistan, and Bangladesh. Many people in these countries are farmers, and their whole way of life is geared to the monsoon. They plant their crops, such as rice, when the monsoon rains arrive in June. The plants grow quickly in the hot wet conditions, and are soon ripe. Harvesting takes place in April or May at the end of the cool, dry season. The seasons allow the farmers to grow a wide variety of crops, such as rice, corn, and fruits.

But there are still problems. In some years the monsoon winds arrive late. When this happens people begin to worry that they will not have time to grow enough food. Everyone watches the sky closely, looking for the dark thunder clouds that will bring the life-giving rain. In other years the monsoon rains are not as heavy as normal. This is a problem for farmers who need lots of water for growing crops like rice. If the harvest is poor because of light rain, people may go hungry.

Heavy monsoon rains can bring different problems. Sudden heavy downpours cause rivers to swell and burst their banks, flooding farmland. Bridges may be swept away and animals and people trapped on higher ground.

So people with monsoon weather pay close attention to the weather forecast. Their governments spend a lot of money on hurricane and typhoon shelters and on space **satellites** to watch the changing weather patterns.

Rice seedlings have to be planted in partly flooded fields.

Temperate weather

Temperate places are those parts of the world that separate hot tropical areas from the cold polar lands. The temperate areas lie between 30° and 60° north and south of the equator. The word "temperate" means mild, and some temperate areas do have a mild climate. However, there are big differences in the weather in temperate areas – from the cold climates of places like Siberia and northern Canada to the cool climate of Britain and the warm climate of the Mediterranean.

Siberia and parts of Canada have a cold temperate climate. In winter, temperatures can fall below 0°F, causing severe problems for people who live in these places.

South Island in New Zealand has a temperate climate.

Siberia

Siberia is the largest area of the world with a cold temperate climate. The winters are very cold, but the skies are often blue and the sun shines. Little snow or rain falls in winter but what snow does fall stays on the ground a long time. Once summer arrives, clouds build up and rain falls.

In the summer, the top layer of the earth thaws out, but the soil beneath it stays frozen. This makes it difficult to build houses, drill oil wells, or mine coal.

However, Siberia has many untapped resources in the ground, and now more and more people are moving into the area in search of **minerals**.

Drilling for oil is a problem in the long cold Siberian winters.

Snowfields and glaciers survive all year round in northern Canada.

The oil in tractors, trucks, and cars can freeze while steel can become brittle and snap. People have to keep themselves well protected against the bitter cold. Rivers freeze solid for several months in the winter, so shipping comes to a halt. In some places the rivers are used as roads because they have frozen so hard. The spring thaw finally arrives around May and the ice starts to melt. Although winters are very cold, summers are quite warm as temperatures climb to about 60°F or higher for three or four months.

Countries that have cool temperate climates are warmer than areas like Siberia. Places, such as Britain and British Columbia in Canada, that lie between 45° and 60° north or south of the equator on the west sides of **continents**, have this cool temperate climate.

In cool temperate places, the weather can change quickly. On a spring day, rain in the morning can be followed by sunshine at lunchtime, **hail** in the afternoon and thunder in the evening! The rapid changes in the weather occur because of **depressions**, or areas of low pressure that pass across land and sea.

In a depression different types of air meet and form **fronts**. At a cold front, cold air pushes under warm air and this usually brings cloud and heavy rain. At a warm front, the warm air overtakes and rides over the cold air, which brings drizzle and light rain.

Sometimes areas of low pressure are replaced by areas of high pressure, called **anticyclones**. These bring dry weather, with sunshine in the summer but cold and fog in the winter.

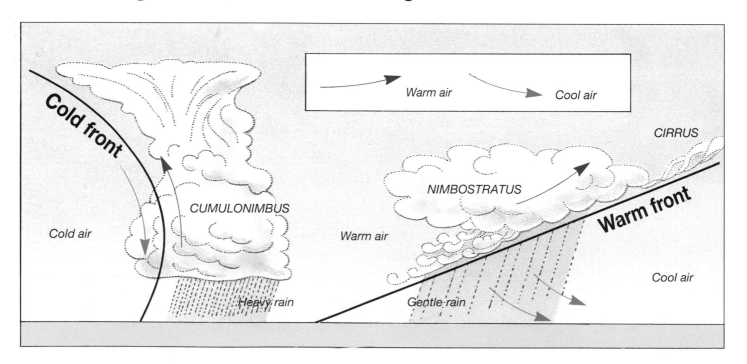

Cirrus clouds are the telltale signs of an approaching depression. Gradually the cloud thickens and rain falls as the warm front passes. A short dry spell ends with clouds and heavy rains marking the arrival of the cold front.

The weather satellite photograph shows sunshine over Britain and Europe and clouds over Russia.

Britain's weather

In Britain all seasons have some rain, but most falls in the winter. High mountains in western Britain get the heaviest rainfall, while eastern Britain is drier. Winters are mild with temperatures between 32°F and 45°F, while summers are warm with temperatures of 60°F - 68°F. These figures are average temperatures.

In the winter the south and west of Britain are warmer than the north and east. In the summer the south and east tend to be hotter than the north and west. Britain's weather is affected by winds that blow from different directions. Southwesterly winds bring mild, damp conditions. Winds blowing from the east and north bring dry cold weather in the winter and hot sunshine in the summer.

Hot, dry summers make places like Barcelona, in Spain, major vacation centers.

Places between 30° north and 30° south of the equator on the western side of continents have a similar weather and climate. This type of climate is called a Mediterranean climate after the most famous part of the world with this type of weather. Mediterranean areas of the world have mild (45°F) but wet winters, and hot, dry sunny summers (75°F). Nearly all the rain falls in the winter months. Their winters are mild and wet because of a series of depressions that cross Mediterranean arcas.

In the summer, Mediterranean areas become regions of warm dry air, and days are hot, dry, and sunny.

Mediterranean climates allow grapes to ripen for wine-making.

This makes them very popular with tourists. In summer the visitors come because there is so much sunshine and so little rain. Even in winter tourists from colder places flock to Mediterranean areas because it is quite mild and sunny, and snow and frost are rare.

Farmers in Mediterranean climates have adapted by growing crops like vines, which have long roots that can find water deep underground. The vines can survive a summer without water. In winter some of these farmers plant wheat, because there is plenty of rain, and the wheat can be harvested before the summer drought.

Polar weather

Places that lie in the Arctic and Antarctic Circles near the North and South Poles have weather that is very cold. In the Antarctic, the temperature never rises above freezing (32°F). During the three months of summer in Arctic areas, the temperature rises above freezing before falling back for the other nine months.

Polar winters are long and cold, with temperatures that have fallen to -128°F in the Antarctic. **Blizzards** can last for days or even weeks. For several months in the winter the sun barely rises above the **horizon** and darkness rules the land.

In the summer in Arctic areas, temperatures rise to about 45°F, and some of the snow and ice melts.

Intense cold and permanent snow and ice are a feature of polar weather. These penguins are enjoying the short Antarctic summer.

A polar bear hunts for seals amid the ice and snow of the Arctic.

During the summer, short showers of rain are common, and for a few months the sun does not set. Daylight lasts for 24 hours each day. Six months later it is winter, and for several months the sun never rises, so the days are long and dark.

People have to learn to survive in such harsh conditions. People who live here use snowmobiles and ski-mobiles to travel around, and they have air links with other countries. But they are often cut off from the rest of the world for weeks.

The motorized ski-mobile is an important way of getting around on the ice.

Mountain weather

Mountain areas have their own weather. Because mountains are high they are cooler than the areas around them. Mountains get about 3.5°F colder for every 1,000 feet they rise in height. In tropical regions, mountains like the Andes are cooler than the lowlands, so lots of people live there. In temperate regions like North America and Europe, mountains are colder than the lowlands, and fewer people live there.

Mountain areas like the Rockies of North America have both deep valleys and high mountains. Within the valleys there is a shady side that gets less sunshine during the year than the sunny side. Most farms and towns have been built on the sunny side of the valley, where crops can be grown. The shady valley sides tend to have more trees and fewer crops and are generally less populated.

In summer, mountain areas often have warm, dry, clear and sunny weather. Cattle feed on the growing grass. But winter comes quickly and conditions become cold and frozen. Then cattle are taken down the mountains to be fed indoors or on lower-lying areas where it is warmer.

The Andes mountains in Colombia

The Andes in South America is one of the world's longest and highest mountain ranges. At different heights in the mountains there are three different weather zones. These are called the *tierra caliente* (hot lands), the *tierra templada* (temperate lands), and *tierra fria* (cold lands).

The weather zones of the Andes are a big advantage in places like Columbia because different crops, from coffee to sugar cane, can be grown in each of the different zones.

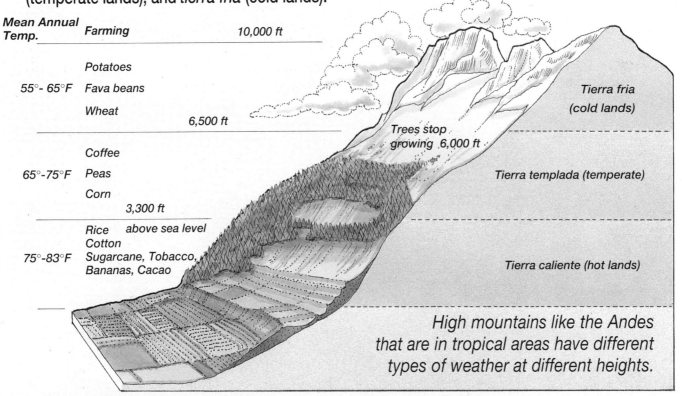

Mean Annual Temp.	Farming		
		10,000 ft	
	Potatoes		
55°- 65°F	Fava beans		
	Wheat		
		6,500 ft	
	Coffee		
65°-75°F	Peas		
	Corn		
		3,300 ft	
	Rice above sea level		
	Cotton		
75°-83°F	Sugarcane, Tobacco, Bananas, Cacao		

Trees stop growing 6,000 ft

Tierra fria (cold lands)

Tierra templada (temperate)

Tierra caliente (hot lands)

High mountains like the Andes that are in tropical areas have different types of weather at different heights.

Often during the night, cold air from the mountain tops drains down into the valleys. This can be a problem because the cold air may damage crops such as fruit and vegetables growing on the valley floor.

Everyone who visits mountain areas is warned about how quickly the weather can change, from bright sunshine to blizzard conditions. The weather in mountain regions can sometimes be dangerous for walkers and climbers.

Forecasting weather

Weather **forecasts** are put together using thousands of pieces of information from all over the world. The information is used to draw charts to show how the weather looks. Then forecasters use the data, their computers, and their knowledge to try to tell us how the weather will change over the next few hours and days.

Weather forecasts are broadcast on radio and television and shown in newspapers. Some forecasts are made for more than a week ahead and are called long-range forecasts. The information used comes from 10,000 weather stations all over the world. Each station records temperature, wind speed, wind directions, clouds, air pressure, visibility (how clear it is), and the amount of rain, snow, or hail.

A meteorologist studying images from a U.S. weather satellite. Satellites make observations of weather movements, which allow accurate forecasts to be made.

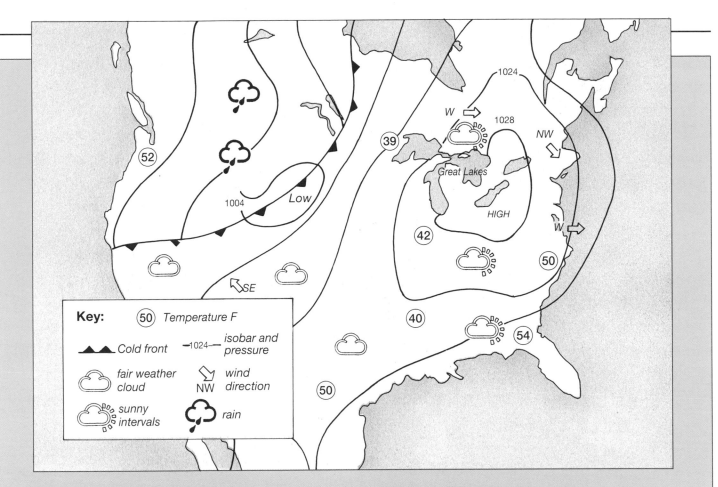

Key:
- (50) Temperature F
- ▲▲▲ Cold front
- ○○ fair weather cloud
- ☁☀ sunny intervals
- —1024— isobar and pressure
- ⬊ NW wind direction
- ☁ rain

The United States, September 21

An area of high pressure lies over the Great Lakes and covers the central and eastern parts of the United States. The weather is fine with some cloud, and light west or northwesterly winds. The figures show that the temperature is lower near the Lakes than on the coast.

An area of low pressure covers most of the western states. The weather is mostly fine with clear skies, but there is cloud and rain close to the western Canadian border.

In this area, winds are light, mostly from the southeast, and it is a little warmer than in central and eastern parts. A weather front crosses the country.

Sunshine and humidity (dampness of the air) are also recorded.

On a weather chart you will see lots of symbols. There may be lots of circular lines. These lines join areas with the same pressure.

The fronts, where regions of high and low pressure meet, are shown with triangles or semicircles drawn along their length. Other symbols on a weather chart can show cloud, rain, snow, and wind direction.

Recording weather

Before weather forecasts can be made, records of weather changes have to be kept.

Rainfall is one of the main things to record. It is measured with a rain gauge. The simplest type of rain gauge is a funnel in a container with measurements in inches marked on the side. The gauge is placed in an open area – away from buildings. The funnel sits above ground level so that water will not splash in and affect the readings.

Wind direction is recorded by **wind vanes**. It is always recorded as the direction from which the winds are blowing. So a southwesterly wind is blowing from the southwest. Wind speed is measured by an instrument called an **anemometer**. Temperature is measured by a thermometer which is kept in a **Stevenson screen**. This screen shields the thermometer from direct sunlight, and so makes sure the readings are correct. You may have an instrument at home called a **barometer** to measure air pressure. It has a needle that moves as the pressure changes.

It is important to keep records every day of the week and set them down in a notebook or on a computer program. The main weather recordings that are made are temperature, wind speed, wind direction, pressure, rainfall, and a description of the clouds.

Weather recording instruments like thermometers are kept in a specially designed Stevenson screen. The slats allow air to circulate but shield the inside from direct sun.

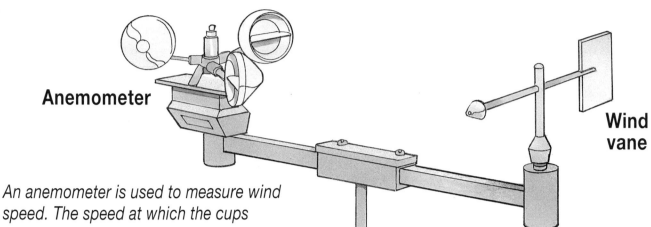

Anemometer

An anemometer is used to measure wind speed. The speed at which the cups rotate shows the wind strength.

Wind vane

Wind vanes show wind direction. The vane always points in the direction from which the wind is blowing.

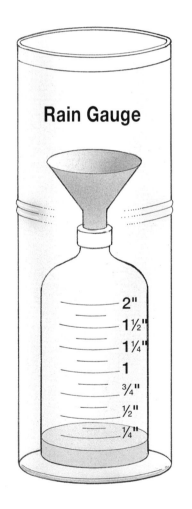

Rain Gauge

2"
1½"
1¼"
1
¾"
½"
¼"

Rain gauges are used to show how much precipitation (rain, snow, hail) falls each day.

Barometer

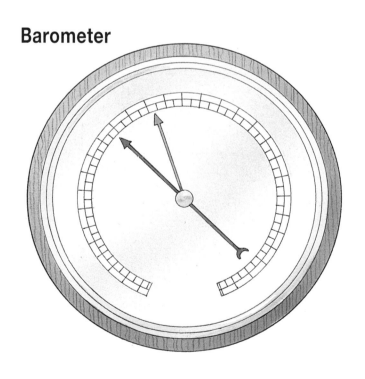

A barometer measures air pressure. Pressure falls when rain is near, and rises when the weather is dry.

Glossary

Air pressure   The weight of the **atmosphere** pressing down on the earth's surface at any point.

Anemometer   An instrument for measuring the speed of the wind.

Anticyclone   An area of high pressure.

Atmosphere   The layer of gases that surround the earth's surface.

Barometer   An instrument for measuring air pressure.

Blizzards   Winter storms, with strong winds and heavy snow.

Climate   The weather of a place on the earth, over a long period of time.

Condense   To turn water vapor into drops of water by cooling.

Continent   A large land mass such as Asia, Australia, or North America.

Depression   An area of low pressure.

Equator   An imaginary line that encircles the earth midway between the North and South Poles.

Forecast   Information that tells us what the weather is expected to be like, based on data from weather satellites and stations around the world.

Front   The boundary between a mass of cold air and a mass of warm air.

Hail   Pieces of ice that sometimes form in high clouds and fall to earth.

Horizon   The line at which the earth and sky appear to meet.

Humid   Full of moisture; sticky, as of weather.

Minerals   Types of rock that are found in the earth.

Satellites   Devices that circle high above the earth. Some are used for monitoring the weather.

Stevenson screen   A white box with slatted sides that protects weather instruments from direct sunlight.

Storm   Violent weather conditions.

Thermometer   An instrument for measuring the temperature of the air.

Tropics   An area on the earth's surface that lies between 23 1/2° north and 23 1/2° south of the equator.

Wind vane   An instrument for showing wind direction.

Books to read

Catherall, Ed. *Exploring Weather*. Exploring
Science. Austin: Steck-Vaughn, 1990.

Davies, Kay, and Wendy Old Field. *The
Super Science Book of Weather*. New York:
Thomson Learning, 1993.

Flint David. *Weather and Climate: Projects
with Geography*. Hands on Science. New
York: Gloucester, 1991.

Gallant, Roy A. *Earth's Changing Climate*.
New York: Macmillan, 1984.

Richardson, Joy. *The Weather*. Picture
Science. New York: Franklin Watts, 1992.

Taylor-Cork, Barbara. *Weather Forecaster*.
Be An Expert. New York: Gloucester, 1992.

Notes for activities

Observe the weather carefully. Identify different types of clouds, and measure elements of weather such as rainfall, temperature, wind speed and direction, barometric pressure, and sunshine.

Record observations and measurements in a systematic way each day over a period of time. These could be recorded in weather pictures depicting the conditions. Such pictures could be changed daily.

Graph the recordings from weather observations; eg. line graph for temperatures or bar graphs for rainfall and wind direction. Use computer programs for recording the weather, if possible.

Relate the weather to other aspects of life. Decide what clothes to wear for different types of weather, what food to eat on hot or cold days, what games and sporting activities to play in different seasons, and so on.

Study the weather in other countries, through television and newspaper reports, and record the weather for places such as in the tropics and the Arctic.

Read stories and poems about weather in other countries, and think about how it affects people's lives.

Index

Picture acknowledgments

The publishers would like to thank the following for allowing their photographs to be used in this book: Bruce Coleman Ltd. 11 (M. P. L. Fogden); John Cleare Mountain Camera 7, 23 bottom (Colin Monteath), 24; Chris Fairclough Colour Library 8; the Hutchison Library 6 (Jesco von Puttamer), 9, 12; J. Allan Cash Ltd. 8 (top), 16; Panos Pictures 14 (Trygve Bolstad); Science Photo Library *cover* (Gordon Gerradd), 19, 26 (Lawrence Migdale); Tony Stone Worldwide *title page*, 4 (Julian Calder), 10, 20, 21 (Christian Kempf), 23 (top); Wayland Picture Library 28 (Paul Seheult); Zefa Picture Library *back cover* (NASA/Dan McCoy), 15, 17 (top and bottom), 22. Artwork is by Stephen Wheele.